Three Ladies of Moreton Bay

Hayles Brisbane Cruises

Mirimar
Mirabel
Mirana

Colin Jones and David Jones

Published by:
Boolarong Press
38/1631 Wynnum Road
Tingalpa Qld 4173
Australia.
www.boolarongpress.com.au

First published 2019

A catalogue record for this
book is available from the
National Library of Australia

ISBN: 9781925877151 (paperback)

Cover image: *Mirimar* departing from Lone Pine in 1966 ahead of two gravel barges (E R Jones photo, C & D Jones collection).

Cover design by Boolarong Press

Printed and bound by Watson Ferguson & Company, Tingalpa, Australia

Three Ladies of Moreton Bay

Hayles Brisbane Cruises

Colin Jones and David Jones

Mirana approaches Hamilton Game Fishing wharf in 1975.
(C Jones photo)

Acknowledgements

We acknowledge with thanks all who have provided photos for inclusion in this book. Particular thanks are due to Brian Martin for his photos, which are a chronicle of the company's later history in Brisbane, but also to the State Library of Queensland, the Queensland Maritime Museum, Picture Ipswich and the Australian War Memorial. Members of the Hayles family, in particular E R (Bob) Hayles in Townsville and Valerie Reid in Canberra, were generous with assistance and anecdote.

The National Library of Australia's 'Trove' digital database of Australian newspapers has been an invaluable resource in fleshing out many incidents and details of events concerning the ships and their environment. 'Trove' is a vital tool for anyone researching matters of Australian and family history and we salute the National Library's efforts in making this available for the benefit of all. Papers and photo albums covering aspects of the whole Hayles operation are held by James Cook University in Townsville as the E. R. (Bob) Hayles Archive.

Most of all we pay deep and sincere thanks to our parents, Mervyn and Heather Jones. Over many years they encouraged and nurtured our love of the Brisbane River and Moreton Bay with excursions on the Hayles vessels to Stradbroke Island. It was, as they saw it, a good and inexpensive family excursion. The many family photos included in this book attest to our gratitude.

Colin Jones, David Jones
February 2019

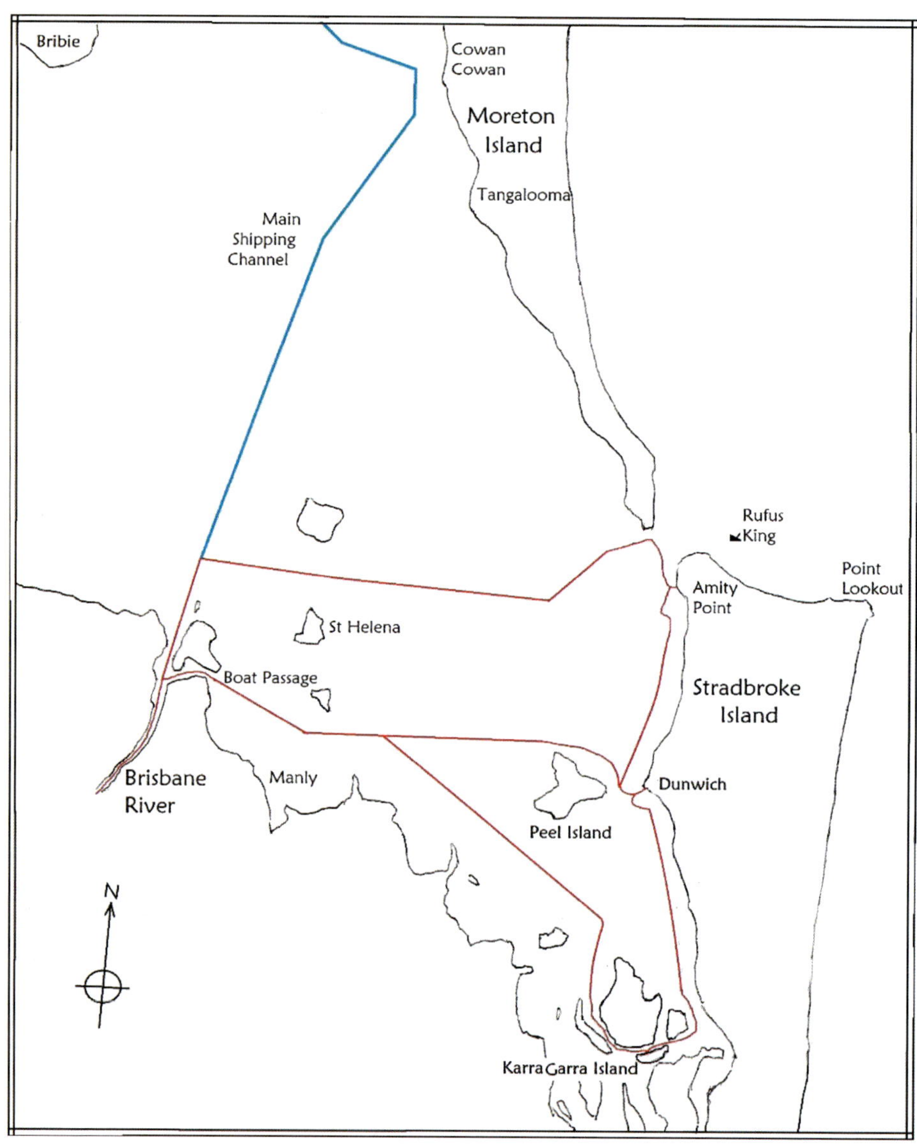

Hayles launches' customary routes in Moreton Bay

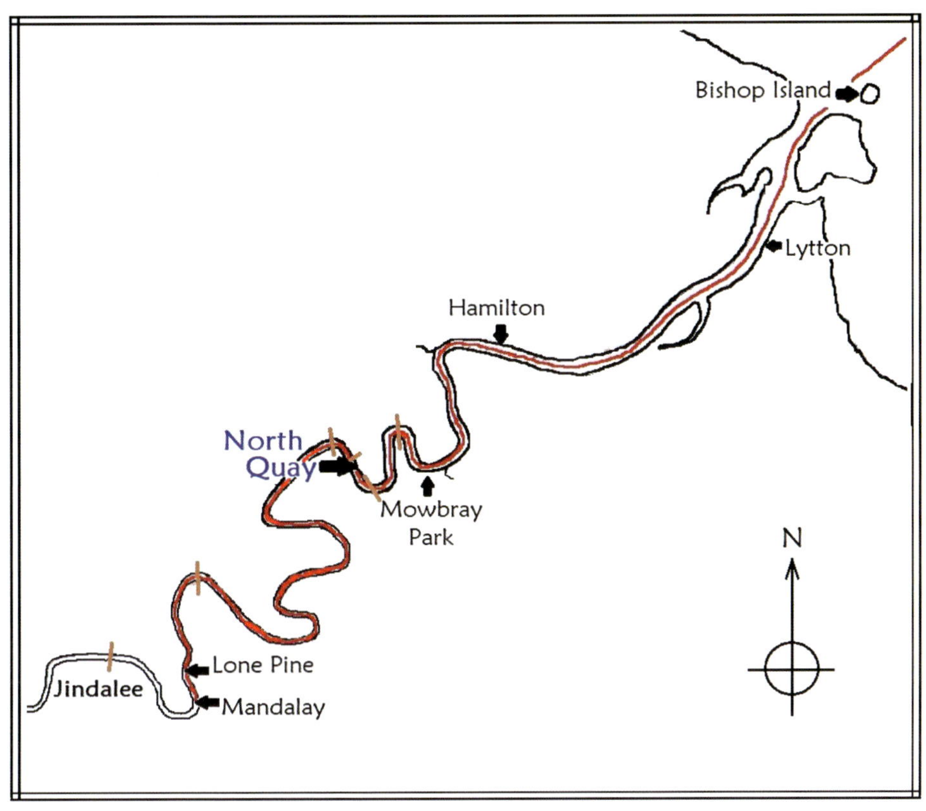

Hayles launches' river routes: upstream from North Quay to Lone Pine and Mandalay; and downstream from North Quay to Moreton Bay

Three Ladies of Moreton Bay

The Hayles company started as a family business in the tourism industry in Townville in 1899, and over subsequent years, expanded, both on Magnetic Island and in running a passenger service from Cairns to Cooktown. The younger Bob Hayles, known to the rest of the family as E R, took over the business from his father in 1916 and the company, Hayles Magnetic Island Pty Ltd, was formed in 1922.

E R (Bob) Hayles and his wife Alison

Bob Hayles became very friendly with Norman Wright, the Brisbane boatbuilder, who built a fine motor launch, the *Malanda*, for him in 1924, with his recommended English Gardner engines. Wright subsequently noted that 'boats owned by Hayles Magnetic Island Ltd were always kept in first class condition by the Company'. It would have been a very friendly and convivial voyage with the Hayles and Wright families taking the latest boat from Brisbane to Townsville.

As a final expansion of the company's interests, a Brisbane branch opened in 1934. Bob Hayles told the press 'There are great possibilities for popularising the islands of Moreton Bay' as he built the 'palatial motor ship' *Mirimar*, at that time the largest motor launch to be built in Brisbane. She also set a new standard as the first excursion launch with covered upper deck seating. Even 45 years later, Bob Hayles was to say that she was still 'the best in the fleet'. The *Mirimar* was built of spotted gum, Queensland hardwood and New Zealand Kauri pine, was launched on 13 June 1934 and christened by Miss Joyce Wright. Her details were as follows:

Mirimar in her early years (courtesy B J Martin collection)

Wood, single screw motor vessel
Tonnage: 77.4 displacement, 69.1 gross, 29.78 net
Length: 90' overall, 82'6" bp, Beam: 18'4"
Depth: 8'5"
Draught: 6'2"
Licensed to carry 240 passengers on Moreton Bay, 300 in the Brisbane River, and 90 outside the Bay.

Maximum speed on trials 10.75 knots, with 228 bhp
One Gardner marine type compressed ignition oil engine, six 11" cylinders with 13¼" stroke.
ON 139376

Mirimar approaching Lone Pine, showing the ladies' cabin for'ard (postcard in C & D Jones collection)

There was a smoking compartment over the engines amidships on the main deck, and a ladies' cabin on the starboard side forward. In the funnel was a soot-catching device so that the ladies would not fear smuts on their light white dresses.

The boat entered service on 6 October 1934, skippered by John Dickson Watts, when she did a cruise to Amity Point, on the north-west corner of Stradbroke Island, where she anchored overnight. Stradbroke Island was front and centre in Bob Hayles's plans for popularising the islands of Moreton Bay. As well as introducing the islands to the wider population, the *Mirimar* carried deck cargo to service the needs of island communities. A derrick was fitted abaft the funnel to handle small boats to go ashore, as well as for light cargo. Among the more unusual cargoes were horses carried on a couple of occasions on the upper deck and slung ashore at Dunwich.

Mirimar unloads cargo on the jetty at Amity, June 1955
(M E Jones photo, C & D Jones collection)

Captain Watts was fined at the start of January 1935 for carrying 300 people across the Bay from Amity, in excess of her licence. He stated that there had been confusion about who was sailing and who was just there to see people off, and there were life-rafts for 300 people nevertheless. Later in January the vessel was caught in a violent storm and had to anchor for two hours with 175 passengers, who did not get back to the city until 1.00am next day.

Subsequent services on Moreton Bay operated on Saturdays, Sundays and Thursdays, with moonlight cruises 'for health and happiness' with an orchestra, Tuesdays and Fridays. The round-trip fare was four shillings.

E.R. Hayles's proposal for lengthening *Mirimar* by six feet in 1938 (presented to C Jones by E R Hayles, C & D Jones collection)

But her speed was a disappointment, as it had been expected to be 12.5 knots. Bob Hayles always required of his boats that they should have a sharp entry forward and a flat run aft. He decided that the flow of water around the hull might be improved by adding six feet to the length of the *Mirimar*, making her 96' overall, and thus increasing her tonnage to 71.02 gross, and 31.09 net. She came out of the shipyard again with this modification in 1938. Also about this time, the men's smoking room was deleted.

Hayles' Brisbane premises were off Queen's Wharf Road, just downstream from Victoria Bridge. There was an office, a passenger wharf with boarding levels for either high or low tide, and a cargo wharf. Crowds would come down the long riverside stairway to join the vessel. The *Mirabel* was given a separate jetty.

Hayles Cruises wharves and office at North Quay. *Majestic* pulls into the main passenger wharf with *Mirabel* in the foreground and *Mirana* at the cargo wharf in the distance. (B J Martin photo)

It was an interesting cruise through the city downstream, with the coastal and overseas shipping to see, as well as houses whose gardens came down to the water's edge, and then out to the broad waters of the Bay. A commentary was provided identifying items of interest and historic sites such as Newstead House and Fort Lytton. A Victorian journalist, writing just after the war described this commentary.

> *An infallible guide is to be found in the person of Captain Frank Smith, skipper of the* Mirimar, *who at the wheel pointed out the many islands around which we were passing, each one redolent of early Australian history. Captain Smith is an enthusiast, who regrets the fact that much of this history, which should be preserved for all time, is being forgotten, due to the indifference of the responsible authorities. He was born, and has grown up, among the islands.*

Captain Frank Smith on the *Mirana* (C & D Jones collection)

Frank Ambrose Smith took over as captain in 1938 and it was said that he could deliver supplies to the men on the Pile Light without even slowing down. He gained the nickname 'two speed' Smith 'because they reckoned I only ever ran full speed ahead or full speed astern'. After turning here towards Stradbroke Island, across the way is the former island prison of St Helena, abandoned in 1933 and now falling into picturesque ruin, and Peel Island leper colony.

As one romantic wrote, 'the speeding *Mirimar* cleaves waters of emerald green on her way'. As you near the South Passage, between Moreton and Stradbroke Island, there are winding passages between the great sands of the Moreton and Amity Banks, first the Rous Channel and then, swinging around Pelican Bank, to the Rainbow Channel. This may sound romantic but it was named for a survey vessel, HMS *Rainbow*. Henry John Rous commanded her when she arrived in 1827. Just so, the first stop, at Amity Point, is a place named for a ship, the brig *Amity*.

Mirimar at sea (C Jones photo)

Amity was a relaxed and undeveloped hamlet for fishermen and campers. Moreton Bay's first pilot station was established here in 1825 but abandoned after heavy loss of life in the wreck of the steamer *Sovereign* in 1848 which proved the South Passage was too dangerous for shipping. This point was emphasised to people in the post-war era who could see the rusted stern half of the Liberty ship *Rufus King* wrecked in the South Passage in 1942.

An observer recorded the scene at Amity.

> *The arrival of the boat is the star event, and excitement is rife. The* Mirimar *disgorges her passengers together with a mountain of luggage and supplies. These are gradually sorted out from seemingly impossible chaos and divided, humans and baggage, into two huge converted military motor trucks. Excitement has by now subsided and no one displays the least semblance of hurry.*

Amity soon found visitor numbers growing as a result of *Mirimar*'s regular arrivals at Stradbroke Island. By Easter 1935 she had been in service for around six months, time enough for Brisbanites to plan to spend the four-day Easter holiday weekend on the island. Really big crowds visited that Easter, including 400 campers and many others came in private boats.

Mirimar at Amity wharf in 1938 (State Library of Queensland image 62936)

Hayles built a jetty at Amity in 1934 but it was in constant trouble due to the erosion of the sand by tides and currents. If you were not careful in the purchase of land here, you might find next year it may not exist. Constantly having to be repaired and extended shorewards, in July 1938 the jetty was washed away. Care had always to be taken that it was not overloaded with passengers. Aborigines from Myora might come up with horses for hire. A shark-proof swimming enclosure of 1937, 90 feet by 50 feet, with a stout construction of old railway rails, likewise did not last long. There was also Hayles kiosk.

On 20 June 1947 there were high seas at Amity with a seven foot tide and some 50 feet of the shoreline was washed away, right back to the edge of the old racecourse. Mr and Mrs Levinge had been living in the old kiosk abandoned by Hayles in 1939 when it was threatened with erosion. It fell into the sea at 3am and the dance floor just floated away. In violent weather in June 1937 the *Mirimar* was unable to berth at Amity and had to return to Cleveland.

Mirana at Amity in January 1972 with engines running ahead against a strong current as she disembarks passengers (C Jones photo)

But the jewel in Straddie's crown was Point Lookout on the island's north-eastern corner. Point Lookout's fishing was legendary and the scenery of its rugged gorges and pristine ocean beaches was stunning. But it was accessible to very few. The *Mirimar* opened up the opportunity for dedicated anglers to reach there over a weekend. Initially some rode their push bikes, loaded with provisions and fish traps around the beach to return home next day aboard the *Mirimar*.

Then in November 1934 *Mirimar* carried a one-ton truck to Amity which would carry people along the beach to Point Lookout. Bert Clayton, after single-handedly building a kiosk at Point Lookout benefited from a road in October 1936 eight miles across the island from Amity. It was just a rough bush track, but land sales at Point Lookout in November were fully subscribed.

Point Lookout ocean beach and rocks of the Bathing Gorge (D Jones photo)

Clayton's bus would take people to the Samarinda Guest House at Point Lookout which he built in 1937 out of driftwood he brought up from the beach. The popularity of this venue saw the building of their own boat, the *Lookout*, in 1939. Significant competition also came in the form of James Crouch's big steam ferry *Gippsland* in 1938. Operated principally as a showboat, with music and dancing, she had a capacity of some 400 passengers and a speed of 14 knots. Her two main cruises were the 90-mile cruise from the city to Stradbroke Island, including the supply run to the 'Government Benevolent Institution' old people's settlement at Dunwich, and an alternative 100-mile Tropical Fruit Cruise to include fruit at Karra Garra Island and the beauties of the Canaipa Passage.

Mirimar at Dunwich in 1955 (M E Jones photo, C & D Jones collection)

The government steamer *Otter* had serviced Dunwich until 1939. In the end, the *Gippsland* proved too large to be profitable and she was taken out of passenger service and returned to Sydney in 1941. Hayles was able to take over the cruises subsequently. Dunwich had been settled since the earliest days as Stradbroke Island's major centre of activity and berthing arrangements were more substantial and safer than at Amity. Dunwich's rock causeway, built by convicts in 1827 had been extended by a timber wharf with a horse tramway connecting the wharf with the main area. When the old people were transferred to the new Eventide Home at Sandgate late in 1946, they were carried on the Hayles launches.

Not to be outdone by the competition, Hayles decided to have a second boat. Norman Wright had designed a larger version of the *Mirimar*, but the decision was for a smaller vessel to take overflow crowds, and also to be available for towage on the river or for charters. So the *Mirabel* was launched in October 1937, owned jointly by Bob Hayles and his wife Alison. Her details were:

Mirabel at Hamilton in 1963 (B J Martin photo)

Wood, single screw motor vessel
Tonnage: 33.54 gross, 14.77 net
Length: 59'6" overall, 53'3" bp, Beam: 14'11"
Depth: 5'1"
Licensed to carry 110 passengers on Moreton Bay and 120 in the Brisbane River

One Gardner 8-cylinder 4-stroke L3 diesel of 136 bhp for 10.5 knots.
ON 159720

Her skipper was C. Alex Swenson. *Mirabel* was just a year old when in August 1938 she successfully salvaged the yacht *Fram* which had been stuck for three days on a sandbank near Amity.

Passengers crowd the Hayles wharf at North Quay waiting to board *Mirimar* for a trip on Moreton Bay

As the trade developed, the weekend excursion to Point Lookout proved extremely popular, though it was said that marriages performed by the *Mirimar*'s captain were good only for the duration of the trip. Apart from the 'effervescent and ever popular' Captain Smith, there could be Eileen O'Donnell to lead the community singing. You didn't want to annoy Captain Smith, however. Once when a young man was sitting on top of the wheelhouse with his legs dangling to obscure the view, he was ordered down. When he refused, some deck hands hauled him down and he was locked in one of the toilets for the duration, much to the amusement of the other passengers.

Our parents in their courting days took a trip down the Bay on the *Mirimar*. Crossing the Brisbane River bar, they were splashed by water coming over the bow. Moving to the rear of the boat to dry out, our mother was sunburnt right though her dress. A wooden canopy was later fitted to cover the whole of the after deck.

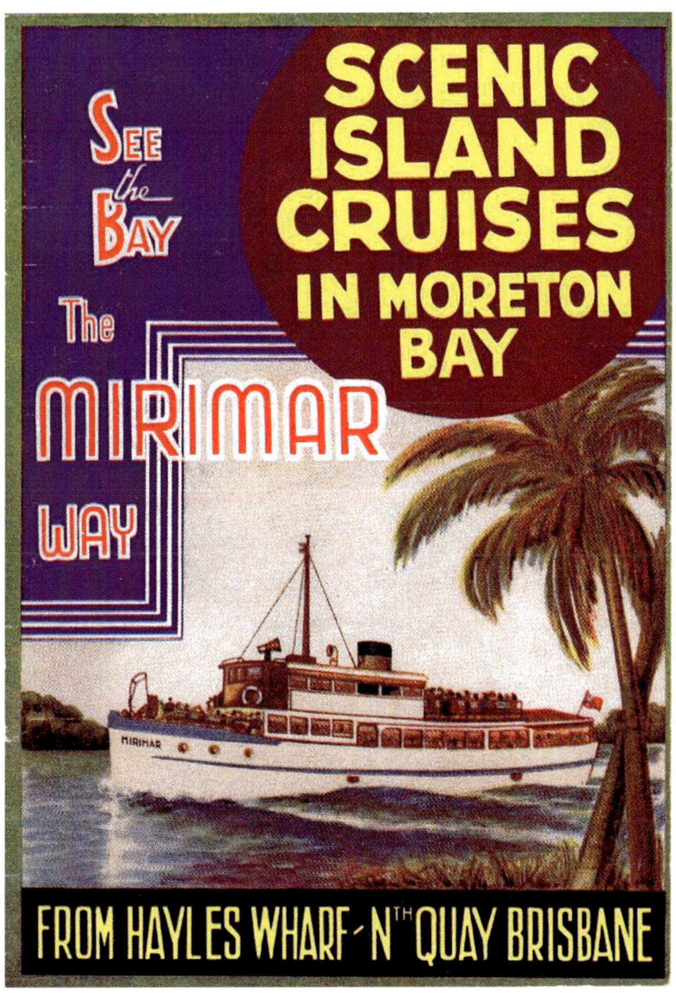

Hayles' publicity brochure made a compelling pitch for seeing the Bay the *Mirimar* way.

> *Being entirely landlocked and possessing a warm climate cruising in Moreton Bay is a pleasure all year round. It is here that holiday makers from the frozen south and the torrid north meet to enjoy the varied delights of this jewel of the Pacific. No holiday is complete without a visit to the southern end of the bay, with its verdant islands set in the most colourful and placid waters imaginable.*
>
> *Hayles Cruises Pty. Ltd. fleet of fast, comfortable and modern tourist cruisers leave regularly from North Quay (next to Victoria Bridge) on scenic excursions to various localities in the southern end of Moreton Bay.*
>
> *The points of interest are described en route, refreshments are served on board and selected musical items are offered during the day, thus holding the interest during the 100 miles of scenic cruising*

A visitor from central Queensland in mid 1936 enjoyed the 100 mile cruise, but when a small boy fell overboard at Amity and was likely to be carried away by the strong current, the engineer E C Evans jumped in to save him. 'This caused rather a lot of excitement for a while.'

The *Mirimar* often followed local yacht racing from the time she entered service. For the opening of the season on 2 October 1934 Mr and Mrs Hayles hosted Mr Pease, the Minister for Lands, and his wife. The boat followed the yacht racing on Bramble Bay for the Forster Cup in February 1939, and in the post-war period she would be flagship. Also in 1939 she took spectators to watch the 12 square metre sharpies sailing for the first leg of the Australian Championships on Waterloo Bay. In March 1953 she took people to follow the cruising yachts out of the Bay on their way to Gladstone in the Easter race.

In 1935 there was a special charter to take 47 members of the National Parks Association to Dunwich for a holiday camping and botanising. Other guests that year included the aboriginal footballers from Cherbourg, and in 1936, a group of NSW sea cadets.

Mirana at Tangalooma in 1963 with a crowd of eager passengers

Less glamorous were Hayles's towage assignments. On 12 May 1952 *Mirimar* and *Mirabel* combined to tow the superannuated suction dredge *Hercules* to be beached near Dunwich as an oyster farm. In following years Hayles launches would regularly pass the hulk on their route from Amity to Dunwich.

Apart from the Moreton Bay services, there was a weekly river trip to Lone Pine and the 20 acre Mandalay Sports and Picnic Ground where Hayles built a kiosk and dance hall in 1937. There were weekend evening 'Showboat' cruises, with music by 'Madge Cloherty's Celebrities'. A Wednesday and Saturday cabaret aboard the *Mirabel* featured 'The Mandalayans' (saxophone, guitar, double bass and piano accordion). Claude Reid's 'Lone Pine Koala Bear Farm' was established in 1927, serviced mainly by his own boat, the *Tourist*, and the permit for Hayles specified that they could not pick up passengers at any intermediate landing places.

Mirabel at Mandalay

All of these busy tourist services came to an end in 1942 with the close advance of Japanese forces to Australia's north. Singapore fell on 15 February 1942 and Australia seemed open to invasion. Moreton Bay became a substantial military area, navigation of the river was limited by a boom at Fort Lytton, and Brisbane started its time as a fortress city. Such was the need for small craft in the Navy that many vessels such as the *Lookout* were requisitioned.

Hayles continued to provide Bay and river trips for the public while filling contract needs for the Army. Excursions were progressively reduced to weekends and ceased at the end of 1942 as military needs prevailed. *Mirimar* and *Mirabel* were taken over by the Army on 19 February 1943 and assigned to the Army's 52nd Water Transport Company. Their gleaming white enamel finish was coated in khaki green, but all of their crews were retained, with appropriate Army ranks. Their masters were ranked as Lieutenants. As a result, they were well looked after, unlike many, such as the *Lookout*, that had gone to the Navy.

Mirabel in Army service as AM114 with another requisitioned vessel at the Customs House wharf in the city during 1943 (Australian War Memorial image 060094)

An engine breakdown in 1944 left *Mirimar* out of service for several months as new parts were built locally for her engines. Hayles Brisbane premises were taken over by the Army from the start of 1943 until late 1945. The residents of islands in Moreton Bay were greatly inconvenienced, though they could obtain permits to be carried on the Hayles boats.

The *Mirimar* had a regular run to service the fort at Cowan Cowan on Moreton Island, as well as the Amity signal station, and for the transport of personnel, provisions, equipment and building materials. Some were quite heavy, such as trucks, Bren-gun carriers and graders. Her captain, Frank Smith, described one of the construction tasks performed for the Army.

A busy scene as *Mirimar* loads stores and construction materials for Moreton Bay fortifications in November 1943. (Australian War Memorial image 3868420)

> *I had been carting all the cement for the construction of the gun casements at Rous Fort* [on the ocean shores of Moreton Island]. *We were taking 60 tons each trip, loading it all on the main deck, as we had to run the ship up on the beach just inside Reeders Point* [the southern tip of Moreton Island]. *To unload meant carrying the*

bags down a 12 inch plank and stacking them on the beach above high water mark. Trucks would run it around the beach at low water to the fort site.

An Army stretcher case is evacuated from Moreton Island to Brisbane aboard *Mirimar* on 13 November 1943 (Australian War Memorial image 4083119)

There were highs and lows in *Mirimar*'s Army service. It was embarrassing to be towed home from Tangalooma after a cable wrapped itself around her screw in a westerly wind. On the other hand *Mirimar* successfully rescued the 300 ton Army cargo vessel *Gundiah* from going ashore on Moreton's exposed ocean beach with her valuable cargo of Cascade lager. The *Mirabel*, for her part, assisted in the salvage of an army floating dock.

Mirimar might also tow a target for the gunnery practice, though this stopped when she was almost hit by a shell. The fortress gunners could not always be relied upon. On 4 March 1942 a shot that was meant to be across the bows hit the minesweeper HMAS *Tambar* right amidships. The *Mirimar* also took firewood to the fort on Bribie

Island, as the cutting of timber there was forbidden for camouflage reasons.

As the war receded northwards, Bob Hayles was vigorous in his efforts to get his boats back and the *Mirimar* and *Mirabel* were repurchased from the Army on 6 August 1945 and returned to their regular runs a week later.

Without a jetty at Amity, *Mirabel* disembarks passengers and cargo to the beach

There was much to be done, but without a jetty at Amity, the *Mirabel* was able to load passengers directly onto the sand, where Tony Durbridge's war-surplus four-wheel-drive Marmion Herrington bus could drive them around the beach to Point Lookout. The *Mirabel* also serviced Bribie Island until the return of the *Koopa*.

The post-war era was a boom time for Hayles. With all its competitors except the *Koopa* and Harry Sullivan's boats swept away, there were big crowds looking for recreation. It was time for a new boat. The company had been restructured in 1946, so for Hayles Brisbane Cruises Pty Ltd, Watts Wright & Co Pty Ltd built the largest of the Hayles' motor launches, the *Mirana.* These were her particulars:

Mirana, newly completed in 1947, on the Brisbane River

Wood, triple screw motor vessel (fully enclosed main deck)
Tonnage: 83.55 gross, 50.78 net
Length: 90' overall, 85'10" bp, Beam: 18'10"
Depth: 7'1"
Draught: 5'5"
Licensed to carry 260 passengers on Moreton Bay with 53 on the upper deck; 300 in the Brisbane River, including 73 on the upper deck.
Maximum speed stated to be 13.5 knots
Two Gray marine diesels of 70 bhp and one Gardner marine diesel of 152 bhp, for 12 knots
ON 191397

Mirana was completed with a semi-streamlined bridge and no funnel. Uniquely among the Hayles boats, the ladies' toilets were aft under a short open deck and the men's, as usual, under the forecastle.

Mirana at Dunwich (M E Jones photo, C & D Jones collection)

Bob Hayles had a reputation in the family of being notoriously parsimonious, and the boat had second-hand engines disposed of by the armed forces. The shallow draught allowed her to navigate the Boat Passage by Fisherman Island in greater tidal states. She was launched at Bulimba on 10 November 1947 and ran her first service on Christmas Day. Her master was Frank Smith. She was flagship for the Albert Cup regatta in January 1950. Also, not untypically, Captain Smith was fined for overloading the boat at Amity in January 1954.

Mirana approaches the landing at Newstead Park in 1983 towards the end of Hayles's Brisbane service (D Jones photo)

Services ran Tuesdays, Thursdays, Saturdays, Sundays and holidays, leaving North Quay at 9am, calling at Mowbray Park and Hamilton Game Fishing Wharf, arriving at Amity at 12.20pm and Dunwich at 2.00pm. The weekend trips went to Amity only, offering the opportunity to visit Point Lookout, and there was an additional 6.00pm Friday departure for Amity, arriving there at 9.30pm. On Saturdays and Sundays there was an 8.00pm 'Showboat' cruise. The homeward voyage during the afternoon was usually a quiet affair after a day in the sun. If the tide was right a shortcut through the Boat Passage between Fisherman Island and the mainland was taken, and a stop at the Game Fishing Wharf allowed some passengers to disembark and transfer to a tram for an earlier arrival in the city

In its time, the 'Mirimar Fishing Club' was very popular. In August 1950, for example, cruising off Tangalooma, Cowan Cowan and Comboyuro, 1,746 fish were hauled aboard by 60 anglers – bream, whiting, flathead and black bream. A new record was set on that occasion by Mark Worthington with 180 fish. In February 1953 the *Mirimar* group defeated a group from Tweed Heads off Tangalooma, to great satisfaction.

When we were young, our family benefited from the cheap fares for a pleasant day's excursion out on the water. It was a bit of a thrill to be on the lower deck in the cafe area and to see waves surging by outside the port-holes.

Majestic pulls into a berth just vacated by the *Mirana* in August 1964 to load passengers for Lone Pine. (B J Martin photo)

Hayles also took over the Lone Pine service, with the *Majestic*. She had originally been the Richmond River steamer *Araucaria* of 1917. Entirely rebuilt with two full length passenger decks, she was the mainstay of the upriver service from 1949 to 1965. Services on the 19 miles to Lone Pine and Mandalay route ran at 2.00pm, with an additional 10.00am service on Sundays and holidays. Visitors were always delighted to be greeted on the wharf at Lone Pine by an Alsatian dog with a baby koala on its back.

Strongheart the Alsatian with a baby koala met each ferry at Lone Pine (M E Jones photo from April 1953, C & D Jones collection)

Charter operations might see two boats sail for Mandalay Tea Gardens, for instance for the Taxation Office annual picnic. Changing tastes in leisure activities saw the Mandalay Picnic Gardens closed in September 1961 but interest in the Lone Pine Sanctuary remained strong.

Mirana and *Mirabel* at Mandalay in 1949 (M E Jones photo)

The matter of speed limits on the river had always been a sore point. The master of the *Mirana* was fined for navigating at 11.5 knots instead of the regulation six knots in the Long Pocket Reach on 14 March 1953. He complained that it was a rule that was widely ignored, including by government vessels, and that at the lower speed he could hardly have reached Mandalay to give time for dancing. The master of the *Mirabel*, likewise, had been fined for speeding in June 1939.

Mirimar passing Brisbane Botanic Gardens after her 1952 update (postcard in C & D Jones collection)

By 1952 it was time to update the *Mirimar*. She had engine trouble in February that year and had to be towed home by the *Mirabel*, so her engines were entirely replaced, giving her the greater speed she needed. In later years the old pistons could still be seen lying in the bilges as ballast. Her internal arrangements were completely modified at the same time, to have a more open main deck and a lower deck café, more or less uniform with the *Mirana*. She re-entered service on 27 September 1952. Whereas her original cost in 1934 was £11,000, the inflation of the Korean War saw her renovation in

1952 cost £10,000. The cost of building the *Mirana* in 1947 was £20,000, the same as the cost of the much smaller *Mingela* in 1951. The *Mirabel* was also modernised in 1966. Demand was often great enough for both big boats to be filled for the Bay services, right through to at least 1960.

Mirimar at the Tangalooma whaling station in July 1954
(M E Jones photo, C & D Jones collection)

While the whaling station at Tangalooma on Moreton Island operated during three months a year in the mid 1950s, in the winter the *Mirimar* would run excursions so people could see how everything worked. The old whaling station is long closed and the area is now a major tourist development. Sand mining commenced on Stradbroke Island in 1949 and development on the island saw Dunwich become a busy centre for commuter traffic. Hayles introduced a direct ferry service from Manly to Dunwich in 1959 with their 72 foot *Megeera*.

With the withdrawal of the *Koopa* from the Redcliffe and Bribie Island service in 1953, the *Mirimar* took over the northern Bay services three days a week. But patronage there had declined, and Hayles refused to service Redcliffe jetty as it had deteriorated significantly by 1961. Bribie Island was served by a barge service in 1956 and the bridge was built in 1963. Indeed, the nature of people's recreation had started to change with the growth in ownership of motor vehicles, so that the surf beaches on the Gold and Sunshine Coasts were now easily reachable.

The Hayles cruises were a much loved mainstay of life in Brisbane and in 1973 their monopoly was confirmed with the takeover of the Sullivan company. The *Mirabel* had been sold to them in 1970 and now she came back under the name *Bellana*, along with the *Nirvana*, which had once been Hayles's *Magneta*.

Bellana, ex *Mirabel*, at Lone Pine in 1975 after returning to Hayles service (D Jones photo)

The *Mirabel* subsequently reverted to her original name. With this takeover, the company added the 34 mile river cruise to Bishop Island at the mouth of the river, Tuesdays, Thursdays, Sundays and holidays until the lease of the island expired in 1980. An artificial island built from river dredging in the early 1900s, there were many rusting hulks of old vessels to help against erosion. They included the famous paddle steamer *Lucinda* and the turbine steamer *Bingera*. Bishop Island no longer exists, being covered by the expansion of land for the Port of Brisbane.

Nirvana, originally Hayles' *Magneta* of 1914, on Sullivans' run to Bishop Island in 1969 (B J Martin photo)

Competition to Dunwich became more serious with the introduction of the car ferry *Myora* in 1964 operating initially from Redland Bay and later from Cleveland. But tourism in north Queensland was booming, and through some rearrangement of its boats by the company, the *Mirimar* went to Townsville in 1969 to augment the Magnetic Island service. She was replaced in Brisbane by the *Malanda* and then between 1970 and 1976 and again in 1980-81 by the *Mingela*. The *Mingela* ran occasional cruises to St Helena where, as the jetty had collapsed, people went ashore in small boats. Hayles had other boats, such as the *Captain Cook*, its first cruising restaurant introduced in 1979, but it was the end of an era.

Mingela approaches the Game Fishing Wharf in 1971 (C Jones photo)

Hayles always had an eye for meeting demand for charters, and special occasions. When the Queen arrived in Brisbane aboard HMY *Britannia* on 6 March 1963 *Mirana*, dressed overall, took a full load of sightseers to meet her at the mouth of the river. The process was repeated in subsequent visits by *Britannia* and Hayles boats participated in other special events on the river. A final special charter saw the *Mirana, Captain Cook* and *Mingela* all ascend to the head of navigation on the Bremer River at Ipswich. This voyage provided the delight of tree-clad banks in the river's upper reaches, but demanded close attention to tide levels to safely negotiate shallows.

Prices were rising, with the Stradbroke Island cruise increasing in the 1970s from $1.90 to $6.00 and Lone Pine from 90 cents to $5.00 and then $9.00.

Mirana, *Mingela* and *Captain Cook* tied up together in the Town Reach of the Bremer at Ipswich (Picture Ipswich image 207073)

Finally Hayles withdrew completely from Brisbane, with the sale of all its local assets in 1985 to help finance development in the north. Local management had been by employees overseen by the family from Townsville, a situation that was regarded as unsatisfactory. The *Mirabel* had been sold in 1979 as a ferry in the Sydney area. The *Mirana* was laid up in 1980, sold and later became a houseboat.

The last survivor was the *Mirimar* which returned to Brisbane in 1984 and was subsequently purchased by Michael Nye for his Mirimar Cruises. She was altered in 1986 to resemble part of her original appearance and began services in the following year on the Bay and river. The Wildlife Society combined with her to offer 'Batty Boat Cruises' to the fruit bat colony on Indooroopilly Island observing the dusk departure of thousands of bats for their foraging expeditions across Brisbane. *Mirimar* continued on her daily Lone Pine run until 27 May 2009 when she was retired after 75 years of service. Her successor, the new 72 foot catamaran *Mirimar II*, made the return voyage that day to carry on the tradition. The old veteran was laid up ashore, where she suffered years of neglect and deterioration. The last local vestige of the past was the *Mirabel*, which returned from the south and became a houseboat on Moreton Bay in 2012.

In April 2009, just a month before ending her illustrious 75 year career, *Mirimar* makes another voyage to Lone Pine (D Jones photo)

Bob Hayles as an old man lived in a breezy house on the side of Melton Hill in Townsville, with a view across to his beloved Magnetic Island. Critical still of the management skills of the next generation, he could look at his photo albums (now in the library of James Cook University) and remember the good old times. Yes, these were lovely boats and the memory of the pleasure that they brought to so many is worth preserving here.

Sources of Quotes

Direct quotes included in this text come from:

- Pages 6 & 8 – "Lure of Pacific Beaches". *The Age*, Melbourne, 15 December 1945;
- Page 16 – "See the Bay the Mirimar Way", Hayles publicity booklet, late 1940s;
- Pages 20 & 21 – "Log Book", No.54 Australian Water Transport Association newsletter, April 1990.

Conversion Tables

During the period covered by this book, weights and measures followed the imperial system and currency until 1966 was in pounds, shillings and pence.

Linear measurement:

1 inch (1”)	= 2.54 centimetres
1 foot (1’)	= 0.3048 metres
1 statute mile	= 1.6093 kilometres
1 nautical mile	= 1.8519 kilometres

1 knot = 1 nautical mile per hour

Weight:

1 pound	= 0.4536 kilograms
1 ton	= 1016.05 kilograms

Gross and net tonnage are measures of volume rather than weight, the latter excluding engine spaces etc.

1 ton	= 100 cubic feet

Engine power:

1 horsepower (hp)	= 0.746 kilowatts

Currency:

1 pound (20 shillings in 1 pound, £1)	= 2 dollars ($2)
1 shilling (12 pence in 1 shilling, 1/-)	= 10 cents (10c)
1 penny (1d)	= 1 cent (1c)

Direct financial comparisons are misleading due to the effect of inflation over many years. In particular, there was double-digit inflation in 1951 and 1952 and also from 1974 to 1977 and 1981 to 1983.

Index

About the Authors

Colin and David Jones were born and brought up in Brisbane where they gained a life-long interest in shipping, observing vessels on the river and going on family excursions on Moreton Bay. Both have retired after careers in the Public Service, Colin with the Commonwealth Government in Melbourne, and David with the Queensland Audit Office. They have continued to pursue their interest in maritime history by research, writing and public speaking. Colin is involved in the World Ship Society, Victoria, and David volunteers at the Queensland Maritime Museum. With their wives, Robyn and Heather respectively, they gain much enjoyment from their families and grandchildren, and in travel.

Maritime books published by Colin and David are:

Patrol Boat Story, by Colin and David Jones (1972)
The Whalers of Tangalooma, by David Jones (1980)
Ferries on the Yarra, by Colin Jones (1981)
Australian Colonial Navies, by Colin Jones (1986)
Wings and the Navy, by Colin Jones (1997)
Steamboat Memories, by Colin Jones (2001)
US Subs Down Under, by David Jones and Peter Nunan (2005)
re-published as *Subs Down Under* (2011)
Wings on the River, by David Jones (2007)
Master Mariner, by David Jones and Peter Nunan (2009)
Royalty & the River, by David Jones (2012)
More Than a Haircut and Shave, by David Jones & Peter Nunan (2013)
The Lady of the Water, by Colin and David Jones (2015)